WOMEN IN POLICING

FIGHTING CRIME AROUND THE WORLD

MICHAEL FOONER

Coward, McCann & Geoghegan, Inc.
New York

CONTENTS

ADAMS STREET

5/77

Library of Congress Cataloging in Publication Data: Fooner, Michael.
    Women in policing. SUMMARY: Text and photographs examine policewomen who are working in all
phases of police work throughout the world.   1.   Policewomen—Pictorial works—Juvenile literature.
[1.   Policewomen]   I.   Title.   HV8023.F66   363.2   76-15571

Photo Credits:
From Interpol offices: Brussels 1, 15(below), 21(top R), 28; Canberra 12, 23; London, New Scotland Yard 5(top), 10, 18, 19,
21(top L), 32(below), 39(top), 41(below), 44(top L), 47(L); Mexico 14(L), 34(C), 38, 44(top R); New Delhi 9(below), 21(below
R), 31(top R), 34(below), 40(L), 43(below), 44(below C); Paris 44(below R); Vienna 45(L), 46(L). Police departments of: Chicago
32(top), 37(below R): Dade County, Fla. 22(R), 37(top R); Israel 21(below L), 29(below), 35, 43(top); Lakewood, Col. 37(be-
low, L); Miami, Fla. 4, 8, 22(L), 46(R); San Paulo, Brazil 9(top), 20(top R); Washington, D.C. 15(top), 31(top L), 36(below
R); Sheriff, Jones County, So. Dak. 39(below), 45(C); U.S. Secret Service 40(R). From: Berlin Press Information office 20(below
L); Chinese Information Service 14(R); Hong Kong Govt. Information Service, 7, 34(top); International Federation of Senior
Police Officers 45(R): Japan Natl. Tourist Organization 13, 20(top L), 44(below L): Motorola Communications Div. 13(below);
Swedish Information Service 3, 20(below R); Police Foundation jacket, 5(below), 11, 23, 24(below), 25, 26, 27, 29(top),
37(top L), 41(top), 47(R). All other photos by Michael Fooner.

A Funny Thing Happened in Sweden . . .

...one summer. Fifty policemen signed a petition demanding, "Get the women out of the patrol cars!"

It was funny, first, because Sweden is one of the most equality-conscious countries in the world, especially in employment, and the police forces are no exception. And second, it was funny because. . . .

Just the previous summer, women police had participated in one of the most sensational "shoot-'em-up" bank robbery attempts in Sweden's history.

Two heavily armed robbers invaded a Stockholm bank and seized four hostages. They threatened to kill the hostages unless they were given 3,000,000 kronor (about $650,000) in ransom, a fast car, and a secure passage out of the country.

The whole city held its breath. As they watched to see how the police would handle the crime, people around the world wondered if this act of terror would be successful. One policeman was shot. But in the end the hostages were saved, the robbers captured, tried, and sentenced to prison, and the Swedish police acclaimed for their skillful, patient, and humane handling of the crime.

Female officers were among nearly a hundred police taking part. One of them can be seen in the picture above, crouching with her weapon in the shelter of a police van, outside the bank where the robbers had holed up with machine guns and bombs.

Nevertheless, a year later a group of male members of the police force signed a petition saying they thought women were not capable of performing all types of police work and should not be assigned to patrol cars.

However, the majority of policemen disagreed. The argument was brought before the policemen's union, and a vote

was taken. The petition signers lost. During the debate another funny thing happened. The attorney general of Sweden spoke in favor of females and said, "In fact, we need more women policemen!"

Did anyone laugh when he said, "women policemen"? We don't know, but it's interesting how habits of speech and thought continue even after customs change.

Meanwhile, in the U.S.A. . . .

. . . a two-centuries-old "men only" tradition has been broken. All over America, women go to work as cops. The same is happening in even older societies, such as those of Japan and India, Germany and France, Singapore, Spain, China, and Poland.

These are interesting and important developments, for interesting and important reasons.

What has happened in Sweden—the debate over women in police work—has occurred in many countries around the world. People everywhere are deeply concerned over what to do about crime and punishment, about the prevention of crime and the treatment of offenders.

These problems are complex; many answers have yet to be found. Meanwhile, the idea of women getting into police work has been catching people's imagination. This book tells what's happening, what it's like having female cops in your town and what it's like being one.

. . . And at Scotland Yard

The name "cop" originated about a century ago at Scotland Yard in London. When a thief was caught, it used to be said he was "copped," so thieves called them coppers. However, since the force was founded by the British statesman Sir Robert Peel, law-abiding Londoners called them bobbies.

As time went on, Scotland Yard became the legendary symbol for democratic police systems, for fairness and efficiency in the fight against crime. But it was a strictly male legend, an image of strong, dignified men safeguarding the community and keeping the peace.

When women were first permitted to join, as regular members, some people were surprised. But now the favorable image of the Yard seems to be even stronger, more modern.

And habits of speech do change, too. With females on the force, hardly anyone calls a London police officer a bobby anymore.

What's in a Name?

After centuries of exclusively male police, people around the world need time to get used to females in the job. In the United States many a man has been perplexed, saying he was given a traffic ticket by a "lady cop" or, in Mexico, by a member of the Policía Femenil. Along with the modern look of the police, new language will probably develop. "Bull" is old-fashioned, and "female fuzz" makes no sense. The French may have a problem, since the traditional *gendarme* derives from a name that meant "gentleman-at-arms."

As recently as April, 1975, an American magazine, the *Ladies' Home Journal,* published an article titled "Police-Women: How Well Are They Doing a 'Man's Job'?" But children in many families say to their playmates, "My mommy's a cop," and it seems natural to them.

The New Look

In Canada there used to be a slogan, "The Mounties Always Get Their Man," but now with women officers in the Royal Canadian Mounted Police, if one of them "gets her man," does it mean she got married or caught a crook? That traditional slogan has passed into history, along with the image of red-coated men on horseback. The modern Mountie rides the frozen north in a jeep, or the city streets in a squad car, and may be male or female.

A Startling Idea

In many countries there used to be strong arguments about having women and men in the same police organizations. There were also disputes about which police jobs were "proper" for women. For instance, in New York City, about 130 years ago it was considered a startling reform when female jailers were hired to watch over female prisoners. It was so startling that officials opposed extending it to police station lockups where those arrested were held before being taken in front of a judge. In the 1880s more than 14,000 females of all ages were held in police station cellblocks at one time and watched over by male officers. Stuffy officials said it would not be "nice" for decent women to come in contact with "the other kind," those accused of disorderly conduct, prostitution, or serious crimes.

Then someone realized that in mixed cellblocks, watched over exclusively by males, there was opportunity for immoral behavior or abuse of female prisoners. So New York then began hiring full-time police matrons.

Today the public in many parts of the world has become used to seeing women patrolling their city streets, doing detective work, or making arrests. The women pictured here are regular police officers on patrol in downtown Hong Kong.

The Things Women Police Do

Some people wonder, What do women police do? Answer: About the same things men police do. But many people are not entirely aware of what the police job is.

Among the everyday tasks of a police officer on patrol (above) are: Helping citizens and getting to know the neighborhood, and handing out a summons for a violation of law, requiring the citizen to appear in court a number of days later.

While women and men police generally do the same things, women in some countries are given specialties, often reflecting cultural variations or needs. In India female police often work on crowd control at festivals, demonstrations and strikes when large numbers of women take part. Still another important task they have is enforcement of laws against slavery, the buying and selling of females to work in factories or brothels. Another job, (facing, above) is checking luggage of female travelers for illegal articles. While prevention of traffic in human beings is a special (though not exclusive) task of women police in India, control of auto traffic is their specialty in Israel. In some countries, as shown (facing, below) in Brazil, women are very often assigned to emergency services and help save lives during natural disasters. In Italy they have been assigned to consumer protection, the enforcing of laws to control prices and shop licenses. Such specialties are in addition to the usual task of street patrol and investigations.

8

How Dangerous?

"We heard shots," begins a true story in *Coed*, a youth magazine published in America, describing what it's like being a police officer.

"The car radio came on and directed us to a bar. Four men ran out, carrying shot-guns. We jumped out, guns drawn, and yelled, 'Freeze! Police! Drop your guns!' They stopped, and we got them up against a wall. We searched them, took them in, and booked them on charges of robbery and weapons possession."

That sort of thing can happen any day, in New York or any other place. It was different this time because one of the police taking part was a female.

Her partner was a male, and when interviewed, he said, "She did her part, the way it was supposed to be done." Both got equal credit for "making a good collar," police jargon that means carrying out an efficient arrest of suspects for a serious crime.

Asked if her job is dangerous, Police Officer Parker—known as Alicia to her family and friends—said, "As a police officer you're trained. You know what to do." Actually, *most* police work is not dangerous at all. Most calls are service calls such as getting an ambulance for an accident victim or freeing a child who's locked himself in the bathroom. When there is danger, she's likely to be safer than other females, because she's trained and has fellow police officers for backup in emergencies. Here (shown above) police are making an arrest of a person behaving dangerously. Looking from crime clues and evidence (left) under difficult and dangerous conditions takes training and experience.

But what about unavoidable violence? Police experts say such situations are the exception, not the rule, and when they happen, women police handle them about as well as men. Experts say it is often not necessary to meet force with force and that women are good at defusing potential violence before it erupts.

How It First Began

The first appointment of a woman as a *regular* police officer was in Stuttgart, Germany, in 1904. In the United States the first was in Los Angeles, in 1911. In London, Scotland Yard got its first regular female police officer in 1915. There were women appointed in New York in the 1840s to work in jails and in the 1880s to work as police station turnkeys, but they are not regarded as having had regular police jobs. New York got its first regular policewomen—and called them that—in 1918. Around this period and in the early 1920s some other countries did the same, England and Scotland, for instance. With many men in military service during World War I, there was a shortage of men for police work.

The first female "international cop" made her appearance in Finland, in 1954, as chief of the Helsinki bureau of Interpol. The first countries to have substantial numbers of women in police forces were: China, where in 1923 the Nanking police department formed a policewomen's force which they began by recruiting and training forty women; India, in the state of Madhya Pradesh, 1959; Israel, starting about 1960; and Austria, about 1965. As far as is known, the first Arab woman to become a regular police officer was appointed in Israel; Middle East countries generally do not call upon women for police work.

More landmarks: The first female regular homicide detective was promoted to that position in Houston in 1961. In 1968 Indianapolis was the first city to give women regular patrol car assignments, and in Canada, female Mounties joined the force in 1974. By the 1970s women doing police work, as in Queensland, Australia (left), and Tokyo, Japan (below), were no longer a novelty to the public.

How It Begins Today: Training

Modern training methods reveal how far women have come in police work. After World War I, when numbers of women began to get jobs as regular police officers, it was mainly for special tasks. Big cities were concerned about the increasing delinquency among young people, runaways, the increase of prostitution, and child neglect.

Police departments assigned female officers to handle those problems and emphasized social service training. Many departments established women's bureaus for offenses by females, juvenile problems, and family conflicts. Even more commonly, women were assigned to clerical work, switchboards, and other tasks requiring no special training. But in the decade of the seventies this began to change, and regular police type of training is more generally given female officers.

In the United States, Canada, Europe, Japan, and other countries the trend is toward giving women and men the same training, from police law to firearms. In places such as the Republic of China and Mexico (above) women have their own classes; in other countries it's coeducational. In Hong Kong each trainee, male or female, gets a free room, plus a servant to clean up and polish equipment.

15

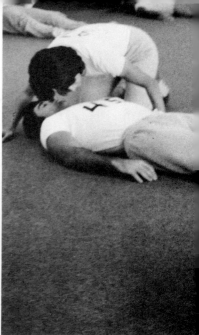

In Mind and Body

Training female and male police together seems more economical. Some say all get better training that way; some say it's a symbol of equality on the job.

Basic training for complete police service covers not only book learning and pistol shooting, as on the previous page, but also first aid for accident and medical emergencies, body building, and self-defense. Shown above is a coeducational class in first aid, while on the facing page, upper left, the recruit finds it's not as easy as it looked at first. In the upper right picture she is working on self-defense technique, and in the center she is getting the hang of it. In the lower right picture she learns "cuffing," how to slip handcuffs on a prisoner.

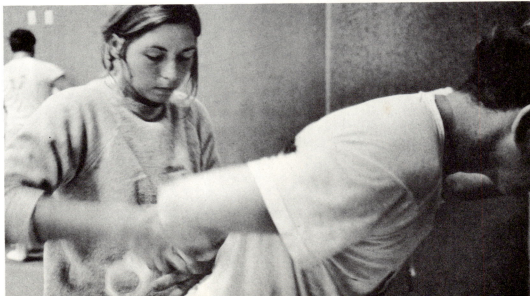

18

Theory and Practice

Training moves out of the classroom and gymnasium and from theory into practice, using real-life situations. Opposite, a woman uses what she learned in a self-defense class against an "attacker." And above, officers are getting advanced training in crime scene investigation. A team is practicing the questioning of suspects and witnesses, while classmates observe their technique.

Many countries have special colleges and academies for police— these pictures were taken at Bramshill Police College in England. In other countries, police departments have both their own training academies and continuation courses at regular colleges and universities. In the United States more than 500 colleges and universities have departments or divisions of law enforcement and police science.

19

Japan

Brazil

The Many Faces of Law Enforcement Around the World

Germany

Sweden

England

Belgium

Even in uniform, individuality is evident, in the faces here and on other pages. Women of many personalities are drawn into this work, and their reasons for joining vary. But from one country to another several aspects of the work are much the same. First, it's a job where the pay tends to be relatively good and has been getting better. Second, people everywhere are concerned about having an orderly life, feeling safe, being treated fairly. Laws are written on these matters, but people are needed, to see that they work properly. Women are interested in being part of this.

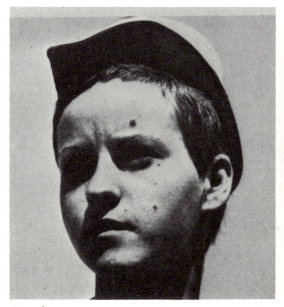
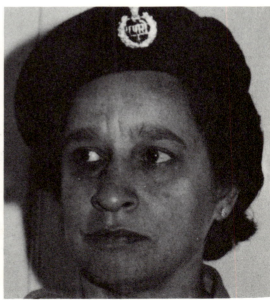

Israel

India

Detectives

Detectives are considered to have the glamor jobs. Actually the work calls for being a Jack-of-all-trades—or a Jill, in the case of females. They gather information from all sorts of places and analyze it, identify criminals and victims, and locate stolen property. They also have to become adept at rules of evidence and at giving assistance to prosecutors. Usually they work in plain clothes, as shown here: developing leads by telephoning, handling evidence at the scene of a crime, getting ready to question a crime witness.

But they also sometimes work in disguises, called undercover, dressing and pretending to be a criminal or a potential victim. Women officers are particularly sought for this type of detective activity—they usually don't look like cops. One named Kathleen, in New York City, has played the role of housewife, Swedish nurse, Southern prostitute, and youth gang groupie at various times, to arrest drug pushers, purse snatchers, and muggers. Another, "Muggable Mary," was responsible for 300 felony arrests in two years on the city streets.

Using women in detective work is an old idea, started long before police departments were willing to accept them as regular officers. As early as 1893 Chicago had at least one female on patrol, assigned to assist male detectives on difficult cases where women and children were involved. Portland, Oregon, had a woman operative in 1905, on duty at the Lewis and Clark Exposition, to see that women and children visitors were not molested. New York had a matron in 1912 who solved a bank robbery and so many cases involving swindles by fortune-tellers that they promoted her to acting detective sergeant. Scotland police—no connection with Scotland Yard, which is the London police force—promoted a female to "regular" detective sergeant in 1926. In the 1950s the head of Scotland Yard praised women highly for their skill as detectives.

However, they got such jobs as the exception. Then in 1970 the West German state of Rhineland-Westphalia began putting women officers into general detective work, French national police appear to have started also, and the idea has taken hold elsewhere. British police employ women detectives extensively, and in the United States a survey in 1971 of twenty-five cities found twenty-one were assigning women to criminal investigation.

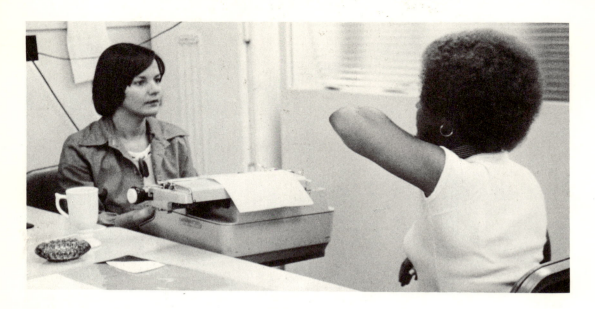

Criminal Investigation Has Its Human Side . . .

A great deal of police investigation, most of it, in fact, is based on contact and communication with people; getting complete and accurate information about a crime from victims and witnesses is a big part of the job. Above, a detective is questioning a rape victim; below, an assault victim. The detectives have to be considerate of people's feelings, as well as thorough and accurate in preparing records and reports. Many police experts believe women often have special aptitudes for this type of responsibility and for understanding the feelings of a person involved in a crime, as victim or offender. Good records are vital to solving cases and prosecuting criminals.

. . . And Technical Side

Investigations of crimes, accidents, and suspicious persons or situations require training (sometimes quite technical) and experience. Above, the officer is making notes at the scene of a highway accident, concerning persons injured, property destroyed, and circumstances that will help decide if the occurrence was wholly accidental or if someone was at fault. Below, the officer is checking physical evidence that will later be sent for tests to the police laboratory.

Patrol Is Basic

Patrol duty is considered one of the basic aspects of police service. Women had to fight to get into it, and when they did get in, it became the symbol of equal opportunity in the police profession. When on patrol, police get close to the people. The community and its police service get a "feel" for each other. The police officer listens patiently to citizens' complaints and differences, as in the two pictures above, or gives a firm warning she hopes will keep a young citizen out of trouble, as shown at center. Below is the sometimes lonely vigil of patrol after nightfall.

Until modern times men, and some women, too, said female police couldn't and shouldn't be assigned to patrol duty—that it was "too rough and tough," they'd "get hurt, run away, be humiliated." But Britain and Israel put women into that type of work and soon afterward announced to the world that they were very good at it. England devised the Beat Constable Team system, which has been adopted in other countries. It's a standardized patrol operation by teams of uniformed officers, with at least one female member in each team. The Israeli police assigned women members to patrol potential trouble spots such as airports and markets and then assigned 500 of them to patrol main roads and frontiers. In the United States, by the early seventies, fifteen out of twenty-six cities with women police were using women on patrol, as were Tokyo and Hong Kong, Rome and Mexico City, Brussels and Vienna, and others.

Making Rounds on Wheels

   In today's industrially advanced countries, patrol in motorized vehicles is practiced extensively. In some places it has almost replaced foot patrol. Motorbikes and scooters have become familiar in some cities and are often preferred for patrol of recreational areas like parks, playgrounds, and beaches. The motorcycle is often used for main highway patrolling and especially to control traffic violations on the open road. Scooters and motorbikes let the officer get closer to the people of the community. Above, left, a Belgian police officer is doing just that; above, police patrol in pairs in Washington, D.C. and left, a squad of female motorcycle police of Mexico are ready to go on duty. Both Mexico and Japan have entire squadrons of women officers patrolling on scooters and in automobiles.

"Car 47 . . . .

Those Swedish policemen who petitioned to get the women out of police cars in 1974 were six years behind the times. Indianapolis assigned two women to police cars in 1968. Because it was a startlingly new idea then, they became famous as "Car 47," and their success in that job was widely reported. Soon other females were put into car patrol, in that city and in other cities. In smaller towns and rural areas that have women police, patrol car duty has become routine. Lakewood, Colorado, for instance, has ten female officers, eight of whom regularly patrol alone in autos.

When women are first assigned to patrol cars with male partners, they are sometimes amused to find the man opening the door for his female partner. Some think it symbolizes less than equal treatment on the job, and men soon skip the "chivalry." Or it happens that sometimes men get overprotective, and when a female signals for assistance, too many male-driven patrol cars dash to her aid. That, too, passes.

. . . Where Are You?"

The motor patrol dispatching system is a nerve center of large police departments, and women are often to be found at the controls. Those shown here keep in constant touch with patrols by radio, to know their location and movements at all times. In recent years, automation and computers have been brought to some cities. Above, left, Washington, D.C., has a system typical of many cities, while on the right there is a contrasting scene in India. Women often work side by side with men, especially in elaborately automated systems like the one, below, in San Diego and in Israel, on the facing page, below.

In The Age of Electronics . . .

. . . Do Not Underestimate the Importance of the Horse

Mobility is one of the key elements in modern police work, but even with all the automated, motorized, and computerized developments in law enforcement, horses are still regarded as invaluable. Their most important use is in crowd control, especially during celebrations, sports events, disturbances, or in congested amusement districts. It is usually the largest and most technologically advanced cities that continue to use horse patrols, and female police officers sometimes find this a congenial assignment.

Beautiful horses are a welcome contrast with the sometimes grim business of the police. These are in Queensland, Australia, above, Chicago, Illinois, facing page, and London, England, below.

When the ranks of the Royal Canadian Mounted Police were opened to women, the official *Gazette* remarked, editorially, "Great horsemanship is one of our famous traditions. Will we have to speak of 'horsepersonship' from now on?"

Traffic Cops

Major cities of the world are heavily motorized and insufferably congested, making traffic control a major problem. China and India, Poland and Argentina, Mexico and the United States are among places where women blow the whistle that keeps traffic moving. Singapore put thirty-five women into a female traffic squad. In Israel, traffic is virtually a female monopoly. When women were first accepted in police work there, they showed special finesse with traffic control and did so well they gained international recognition as the world's best traffic cops. They were asked to train traffic police in France, Great Britain, Japan, and a number of other countries. A familiar sight (above) is a woman officer in the congested "Times Square" of Jerusalem. Women are also in charge in Hong Kong, Mexico, and India, as seen on the facing page.

In Israel, women gained so much prestige in traffic control they were able to press for more jobs in other branches; now the Israeli police force has a greater proportion of women than any other in the world. Women have about 20 percent of the jobs, including detective and narcotics work, communications, criminal intelligence, and prosecution.

Many Jobs, Many Kinds of People

On September 13, 1974, the International Federation of Senior Police Officers, meeting in Germany, reviewed a report of its Study Commission and then approved a resolution which said in part: "Nothing whatsoever has been found to indicate that biological factors handicap the employment of women in any sector of police work . . . they should be engaged under employment and training principles applied to men."

Laboratory Technician

Administration

Public Information

Computers

It had taken a little more than a half century for the police profession formally to reach this point. Back in 1922 the International Association of Chiefs of Police had declared: ". . . crimes by and against females and boys up to age 12 should be their responsibility. . . ." But this view has changed, and the Association's Policewoman's Information Center monitors the expanding role of women in police work. Modern police departments assign women officers to the full range of police work. Why the change? Was crime different in those bygone days? Or do people now realize the old ways of dealing with crime must go, that new ideas must be developed?

Marine Patrol

Fingerprint Technician

Missing Persons

Chief!

The chief of police in Lakeside City, Texas, is a woman; so is the chief in Echo, Oregon. The idea of "room at the top" is getting around. The chief officer in Fairfield County, Connecticut, is the sheriff, and a woman holds that post, while in Jones County, South Dakota, a woman (below, right) is deputy sheriff. The American frontier tradition had chiefs of police or sheriffs chosen by popular election and in many places—mainly small towns and suburbs—the job still goes by ballot. Some women see that as opportunity for them to get ahead.

In many large cities, where most of the jobs are, opportunities for advancement have slowly begun to open. In those cities and in some countries such as Austria, Belgium, and Great Britain, women can compete for promotion on the same basis as men. In some countries a certain number of the higher-rank positions are allotted to females. In Bombay, India, women have two positions reserved as inspector, nine as subinspector, and thirty-nine as head constable. Mexico also has women commanding officers, as shown below. There, as in India and Japan, they are in all-women sections or brigades, but in some places women in higher ranks supervise men. New York City has a female lieutenant in a busy precinct with more than a hundred men under her command; Scotland Yard has had a female as chief superintendent—head of the London metropolitan police force.

Opportunity to advance is often by examination, and this gave rise to a historic legal battle in New York. In 1961 a woman cop there filed a lawsuit for the right to take the sergeant's promotion exam. The city government fought, but she carried the case to the highest court in the state. It ruled in her favor, and she has since advanced to lieutenant. Other women have followed, but the same dispute has still to be decided in many other places.

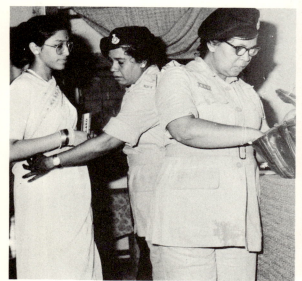

Crime Prevention

Prevention of crimes has become the most important part of police work. The world has witnessed an upheaval in criminal behavior, marked by bombings, hijackings of airplanes, trains, and trucks, kidnappings, assassinations, and the holding of hostages. These are in addition to smuggling, robbery, and thieving, familiar crimes of the past. As a consequence, a growing part of police work is in finding ways to prevent such crimes. Passengers, business travelers, tourists, and visitors to important buildings are now routinely searched for firearms and explosives, for illicit drugs and contraband materials. Here women officers are on duty at an airport in India, and at the White House in Washington, D.C. In a search for drugs an officer is alert to concealment on the person. Women do personal searches of female prisoners. At a checkpoint in England, a police woman-and-dog team search a passenger car for drugs or explosives, with a dog specially trained for this task.

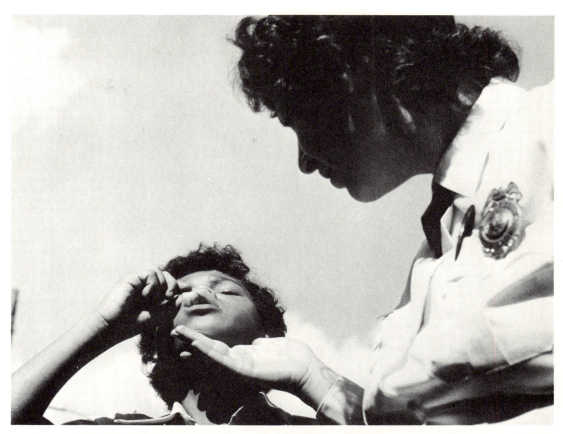

41

Education and Self-Defense

Above, a police officer in New York is teaching self-defense; on the facing page, above, one in Israel is teaching traffic safety; below, police in India are teaching members of a boys' club how to keep out of danger. Police are in a unique position to know the particular hazards of crime and carelessness in each community. In many countries the importance of prevention has been recognized—fire prevention, accident prevention, and crime prevention. Prevention is much the better method of dealing with hazards—it is less painful and less costly. Male and female officers are equally capable of teaching how to prevent crimes, but on some topics, such as teaching rape prevention to girls and women, a female may be better than a male.

Fashion in Uniform

Old English

Mexico

Japan

India

France

Where should a woman wear her gun? On her hip under the jacket or exposed at her waist? In an ankle holster under flared pants? Today most countries want their women police to look like police but also to look feminine. Police uniforms used to be designed only by men, but women are now getting a chance to voice opinions. Skirts or pants? Loose-fit or snug? In India some are dressed in the sari, blue, with badge and shoulder straps, others in bush jackets and pants. What about long hair? In case of resistance to arrest, will it be grabbed? In the United States a city policeman on patrol may carry ten or fifteen pounds of equipment around his waist, counting gun, extra bullets, handcuffs, nightstick, notebook, flashlight—and recently a walkie-talkie radio, too. In other countries he may be less burdened, but should his female counterpart "wear" her equipment or carry it in a shoulder bag? Local conditions and local taste dictate variations, as does climate. Uniforms may range from a heavy jacket in South Dakota to a short-sleeve shirt in Florida. The length of skirts may reflect differences in national style sense. Fashion in each police force strikes a balance to express the personality of the woman, the authority in which she is clothed, and the job to be done.

Austria

United States

Germany

Service to the Community

"It doesn't take a hard-core crime fighter to deal with eighty percent of our calls," according to Miami's former Chief of Police, B. L. Garmire. "But it does take people with compassion, empathy, and ability. Women meet all these requirements . . . and are good crime fighters as well." Most police calls are for services, to handle emergencies, to teach people how to be alert, check the security of property, or for intervention in family situations, to calm tensions and prevent potential crimes.

THERE'S MORE THAN MEETS THE EYE HERE

Police work is continually fascinating. Many people enjoy fictional police stories, "cop shows" on television, and "cops and robbers" movies. In this book you have seen the real thing and read about what's really happening. There's more to read and do and find out.

At the Library: You might try these books:

Abrecht, Mary Ellen. *The Making of a Woman Cop.* New York: William Morrow & Co., 1976.

Fleming, Alice. *New on the Beat: Women Power in the Police Force.* New York: Coward, McCann & Geoghegan, 1975.

Milton, Catherine. *Women in Policing.* Washington, D.C.: The Police Foundation, 1972.

Uhnak, Dorothy. *Policewoman.* New York: Simon & Schuster, 1964.

Visit:

Your hometown or city police department. It's best to make an appointment in advance. Get in touch with the public information officer of the department—write and follow up with a telephone call. If you visit (or live in) Washington, D.C., the FBI has free guided tours you can ask about taking.

Write:

But be specific about what you'd like to know. Address your letter to the public information officer of your local police department or to the public information officer of the state police, in your state capital.

The cooperation of many law enforcement and civic organizations has made this book possible, especially: The National Central Bureaus of Interpol in Washington, D.C., London, Paris, Brussels, Ottawa, Canberra, New Delhi, and Vienna; the police departments of New York City, Miami, and Washington, D.C.; the International Association of Chiefs of Police, Gaithersburg, Maryland; the International Federation of Senior Police Officers, Münster, West Germany; the Chamber of Commerce, São Paulo, Brazil; the library of the National Council on Crime and Delinquency, Hackensack, New Jersey. They and the other organizations listed in the photo credits provided information, or photographs, or both. Their assistance is gratefully acknowledged.